AN OFFERING OF HOPE, PEACE, JOY & LOVE!

ADVENT
AT THE KiDS TABLE
DARYN STYLIANOPOULOS, LIN STORY-BUNCE
KENDALL GRUBB & JUNE BUNCE

THE WELCOME TABLE

CONTENTS

WELCOME TO THE TABLE!

We are so excited that you are joining us for this journey through the Advent season.

As we enter Advent, we are celebrating God's love entering the world!

Advent at the Kids Table is jam-packed with stories, Scripture, and fun ways to bring more hope, peace, joy, and love into your Advent season.

Each day's entry offers a reflection that allows us to meet God in new ways through story and Scripture, helping us to see our own belovedness and gain a deeper understanding of God's big love for the world.

Advent at the Kids Table can be used in tandem with our books *Advent at the Welcome Table* and *Advent Table Talk*, or it can be used independently. The stories in *Advent at the Kids Table* have been adapted from those in *Advent at the Welcome Table*, which allows your family to enjoy the Advent journey together. The Kids Table Talk also correlates with each day in *Advent Table Talk* so that you can dig into deeper conversations with one another. This Advent series is designed to create opportunities for you to journey through each day of Advent in meaningful conversation with loved ones and friends.

Whether you are reading through these reflections by yourself or along with others, we hope you get to know this God who brings to our weary souls renewed hope, abiding peace, resounding joy, and incarnate love.

A WEEK OF HOPE

DAY 1: TINY LIGHTS OF HOPE

SETTiNG THE TABLE

Our days are busy and it can be hard to find time to quiet ourselves and be with God. Take some time to settle yourself. Find a comfortable place to sit. Breathe in . . . breathe out. Do that again. Breathe in . . . breathe out. Close your eyes and remember that God loves you!

This is our first week of Advent, the season of days before Christmas. We are waiting for the birth of Jesus! As we wait, we think about the many ways God is with us in our waiting. This is the week of hope. So this week, we are considering the ways that God's hope is showing up in the world around us.

Above all, watch with glittering eyes the whole world around you because the greatest secrets are always hidden in the most unlikely places. Those who don't believe in magic will never find it.
— ROALD DAHL[1]

JOHN 1:5
The light shines in the darkness, and the darkness did not overcome it.

FOOD FOR THOUGHT

One Christmas, not too long ago, a small city called Aleppo was going through a war. Christmas is usually a time of joy and celebration. Instead, the war made people feel unsafe. Children weren't able to go to school. Families didn't always have food to eat when dinnertime rolled around. And as the weather got colder, parents worried they wouldn't be able to find coats to help keep their children warm.

It is hard to imagine how someone might look forward to Christmas at such a difficult time. It's hard to imagine how the people in Aleppo could find hope when all around them was sadness. Hope is the little tug in our hearts that helps us believe things can be better even when what's happening around us is really sad.

In that same city of Aleppo, there was a friar by the name of Fr. Ibrahim. Fr. Ibrahim loved the people in his city and found ways to help them keep hoping even while going through this hard time. Through small acts of kindness, Fr. Ibrahim and his church brought joy to the city: taking care of those who were sick, providing food to families who needed it, giving coats to children who were cold, hosting a Christmas party so friends could enjoy playing together.[2]

As Christmas grew closer, the people who lived in the city decorated the church with tiny Christmas lights and, at night, all those tiny lights were a sign of comfort to the city. Just like a flashlight or night-light gives us comfort in the night, these lights helped people see the possibility of hope and love in a difficult time.[3]

As you go through this Advent season, pay attention to all the tiny Christmas lights going up on the houses and trees around you—and remember that you are also a bright light of hope in our world.

BLESSiNG

God of Hope,
Help us to remember that our small acts of kindness
can be a light of hope and comfort to those around us.
Amen.

KiDS TABLE TALK

- Talk about the ways that a flashlight or a night-light can help us see and offer comfort at night.

- Think together about some difficult things that might be going on in your family or in your community. How can you be a tiny light or be a big comfort to people who are going through a difficult time?

- Find a tiny light to place in your window throughout the Advent season. Let this light shine as hope for those who pass by. Let this light shine for you as a reminder to embody hope in small acts every day.

DAY 2: PLANTING SEEDS OF HOPE

SETTING THE TABLE

Our days are busy and it can be hard to find time to quiet ourselves and be with God. Take some time to settle yourself. Find a comfortable place to sit. Breathe in . . . breathe out. Do that again. Breathe in . . . breathe out. Close your eyes and remember that God loves you!

This is our first week of Advent, the season of days before Christmas. We are waiting for the birth of Jesus! As we wait, we think about the many ways God is with us in our waiting. This is the week of hope. So this week, we are considering the ways that God's hope is showing up in the world around us.

UNLESS someone like you cares a whole awful lot, nothing is going to get better. It's not.
— **DR. SEUSS**[4]

MARK 4:26-27

The kingdom of God is as if someone would scatter seed on the ground, and would sleep and rise night and day, and the seed would sprout and grow, though he does not know how.

FOOD FOR THOUGHT

Wangari Maathai is a woman who grew up in a country called Kenya. When she returned home from the United States, where she went to school, she discovered that her homeland was being destroyed by people who were cutting down their trees. This caused water and food shortages for her people, as well as malnutrition and disappearing wildlife. In response, she formed the Green Belt Movement—teaching other women and children about the need to care for the land and equipping them to replant forests one tree at a time.

Jesus says the Kingdom of God is like this.

It is like someone who plants seeds in the ground not knowing how or if the crop will grow. She does not know if the ground she prepared will be fertile enough. She does not know if her efforts will prove fruitful or plentiful. Yet she casts her seeds anyway because the possibility of what could come of that seed begs her to do so.

Wangari could not know what would come of her work. Would the trees grow big and tall? Would other people join her and believe that what she was doing was important work?

Still, with the fragile seeds of trees and hope in her hands, she planted both.

Our world needs us to be people who can hold fragile seeds of hope in our hands and plant them boldly. We may not be planting actual seeds, but our words and actions and everyday acts of kindness are seeds we are sowing in the world. It is up to us to plant seeds of hope that change our own lives and change other lives, too.

Our seeds of friendship can make others feel welcomed, our seeds of kindness can grow into more acts of kindness, and our seeds of hope can help us dream and imagine a bigger, more wonderful world for everyone.

In this season of Advent, we remember together that planting seeds of hope and love does not happen all at once, but little by little—one seed at a time.

BLESSING

God of Hope,
We give thanks for the seeds that have been planted in our life—
seeds of hope, of friendship, of love, of belonging—
and for the seeds of hope that we are planting in the hearts of those around us.
Amen.

KIDS TABLE TALK

- Think about or talk together about the miracle of a seed. Consider especially how little a seed is and what it becomes. How is hope like this seed?

- What seeds are you planting within yourself? What seeds are you planting in the world around you?

- Carry a seed (or a picture of a seed) in your pocket today to remind you to plant seeds of hope, and love, and joy, and peace with your life.

DAY 3: HOPE AND LIGHT

SETTiNG THE TABLE

Our days are busy and it can be hard to find time to quiet ourselves and be with God. Take some time to settle yourself. Find a comfortable place to sit. Breathe in . . . breathe out. Do that again. Breathe in . . . breathe out. Close your eyes and remember that God loves you!

This is our first week of Advent, the season of days before Christmas. We are waiting for the birth of Jesus! As we wait, we think about the many ways God is with us in our waiting. This is the week of hope. So this week, we are considering the ways that God's hope is showing up in the world around us.

Wherever you fly, you'll be best of the best.
Wherever you go, you will top all the rest.
Except when you don't. Because, sometimes, you won't.
I'm sorry to say so but, sadly, it's true
that Bang-ups and Hang-ups can happen to you.
You can get all hung up in a prickle-ly perch.

And your gang will fly on. You'll be left in a Lurch.
You'll come down from the Lurch with an unpleasant bump.
And the chances are, then, that you'll be in a Slump.
And when you're in a Slump, you're not in for much fun.
Un-slumping yourself is not easily done.
— DR. SEUSS[6]

ISAIAH 60:1
Take heart; for your light has come,
and the love of the Lord has come upon you.

F●●D F●R TH●UGHT
We don't always get things right.

No matter how young or how old we are, sometimes we make mistakes. We may not always get the right answer on a math problem, or pronounce or spell a word correctly. We might play the wrong note on the piano, or forget the lines in a school play. We might miss the goal when we shoot or kick the ball in a game, or miss the ball when we swing. Sometimes we might say something hurtful or let our anger get the better of us.

It is easy to feel disappointed when these kinds of things happen. It is easy to feel sad about our mistakes. It is okay to feel that way. But there is something you should know about mistakes—they do not define who we are. In other words, there is more to us and our potential than the mistakes we make.

The prophet Isaiah says, "Take heart; for your light has come, and the love of the Lord has come upon you." Take heart is a phrase of encouragement and comfort. It is something that we say to remind others not to be discouraged. It is something we say to encourage someone to keep trying. They are also good words to say to ourselves—take heart!

We all make mistakes, but we also have opportunities to try again. No one is perfect, and everyone has to try again at some point in their life. There is certainly nothing wrong with trying to be a little better than we were before. Every day is an opportunity to practice, to get a little more practiced at something we care about, to be a little kinder, to make better choices. Whatever it is, practice helps, and it is okay to try and try again. That's how we shine our inner lights a little brighter, bit by bit, in the world.

You can do it! Take heart! God loves you and believes in you!

BLESSING

God of Hope,
Help us to know that you love us even when we make mistakes,
and help us to know that we are never alone.
Amen.

KIDS TABLE TALK

- Think about or talk together about a time you made a mistake. What did that feel like? How did you handle it?

- Why is it important to make mistakes? How do we learn and grow from our mistakes?

- Take a moment to look around the room. Then, turn on a flashlight and turn off the room's lights. What do you notice about the room now with your flashlight that you didn't notice before turning off the lights? As you move through the more difficult moments of this season, try to notice the way you experience God's love in new and different ways.

DAY 4: WORDS OF HOPE

SETTiNG THE TABLE

Our days are busy and it can be hard to find time to quiet ourselves and be with God. Take some time to settle yourself. Find a comfortable place to sit. Breathe in . . . breathe out. Do that again. Breathe in . . . breathe out. Close your eyes and remember that God loves you!

This is our first week of Advent, the season of days before Christmas. We are waiting for the birth of Jesus! As we wait, we think about the many ways God is with us in our waiting. This is the week of hope. So this week, we are considering the ways that God's hope is showing up in the world around us.

[You are] the one and only ever you.
— NANCY TILLMAN[7]

MATTHEW 5:14, 16
You are the light of the world. Let your light shine before others, so that they may see your good works and give glory to your Father in heaven.

FOOD FOR THOUGHT

One year when I was a kid, my grandma made each of her grandchildren a gift. Mine was a small rug I could put in my bedroom. The front of the rug had fish with silver, glittering bubbles ascending from the fishes' mouths, some green seaweed, and a yellow starfish. On the back she wrote: "I hope life goes swimmingly always—I always will look for sparkles in your eyes and bubbles in your heart!"

I was a little surprised by her note. It wasn't that I was an unlikable kid— but I was often told that I talked too much and that my hyper energy was exhausting. I had a good heart and cared deeply, but this also meant that I got my feelings hurt easily and cried a lot. And as a rough and tumble girl, I had never really thought of myself as sparkling.

We spend so much time seeing ourselves through the eyes and minds of other people—the eyes of our parents, of our friends, of our teachers. We see ourselves through the lens of "should haves" and "shouldn't haves": I should be a better soccer player. I shouldn't have cut my hair so short. I should try to be more like those kids. I shouldn't let others know that I really like piano. It's exhausting. And all those "should haves" and "shouldn't haves" don't allow us to fully accept or rejoice in who we know ourselves to be.

In Matthew 5:13-14, Jesus says, You are the salt of the earth. . . . You are the light of the world." In other words: See yourself as God sees you. You—just as you are—bring light and joy to this world in a way that only you can. God takes great joy in you!

How often do we take the time to see ourselves through the eyes of God? How often do we see ourselves as an important light in this world?

My grandmother's gift invited me to see myself through a lens of love. On this gift she wrote words of hope that reminded me how important it is to see in myself the very light she saw in me—and the very light God put in each one of us.

BLESSiNG

God of Hope,
Help us to remember that we shine with a light that only we can shine—and that we were made with a spark that only we carry.
May our being and our words spark a light of hope in the world around us.
Amen.

KiDS TABLE TALK

- Can you remember a time when someone said something kind or encouraging to you? How did that make you feel?

- Name one or two things about yourself that make you who you are. Remember that God made you to be exactly who you are!

- Spend today seeing yourself and those around you through the eyes of God. Offer words of hope and encouragement to yourself and others, and see how it adds light and love to your perspective.

DAY 5: HOPE IN UNEXPECTED PLACES

SETTiNG THE TABLE

Our days are busy and it can be hard to find time to quiet ourselves and be with God. Take some time to settle yourself. Find a comfortable place to sit. Breathe in . . . breathe out. Do that again. Breathe in . . . breathe out. Close your eyes and remember that God loves you!

This is our first week of Advent, the season of days before Christmas. We are waiting for the birth of Jesus! As we wait, we think about the many ways God is with us in our waiting. This is the week of hope. So this week, we are considering the ways that God's hope is showing up in the world around us.

LUKE 2:15-20

When the angels had left them and gone into heaven, the shepherds said to one another, "Let us go now to Bethlehem and see this thing that has taken place, which the Lord has made known to us." So they went with haste and found Mary and Joseph, and the child lying in the manger. When they saw this, they made known what had been told them about this child; and all who heard it were amazed at what the shepherds told them. But Mary treasured all these words and pondered them in her heart. The shepherds returned, glorifying and praising God for all they had heard and seen, as it had been told them.

FOOD FOR THOUGHT

Can you imagine what it might have been like to be at that first Christmas? Angels just popping up everywhere in the sky. Everyone in Bethlehem talking about this baby—a baby who was born not in a hospital, but in a barn. People going barn door to barn door just to sneak a peek at this special baby. Mary and Joseph doing their very best to make a crib and blanket out of hay and old clothes.

During the Advent season, we sometimes sing the song Silent Night, but this first Christmas doesn't sound like it was very silent. It seems like it may have been kind of wild, actually—except for one part. While shepherds and animals and curious children were making their way into the crowded stable, Mary, Jesus's mom, was sitting silently beside her baby, paying attention to what was happening around her: the baby peacefully asleep, the sheep helping her keep watch, the shepherds running in from the fields, a busy innkeeper, the visitors stopping by.

Mary cannot sleep because she knows what everyone else feels, but cannot yet understand. She knows that this baby is something incredibly special. That something amazing and miraculous has happened right there in front of them. In the most surprising of places—a barn!—to people who did not expect it. Right there in front of them, the very heart of God was born into the world. A crying, perfect, tiny little baby.

In this Advent season, let us remember together that this is how God's love comes into the world most often: in surprising ways, through ordinary people like you and me, in moments we do not expect—but most certainly in ways that leave us forever changed.

BLESSING

God of Hope,
Thank you for showing up in unexpected places
and for entering our world in unexpected ways.
Amen.

KIDS TABLE TALK

- Can you remember a time that you experienced God's love and presence in an unexpected way?

- Who are some people in your life that help you to better know God's love?

- This week, try to pay attention like Mary. Pay attention to the places where God's love is showing up in surprising, unsuspecting moments. Be open to the ways that a conversation with a friend, the kind act of a stranger, or hearing the perspective of someone who believes differently than you somehow opens your heart, leaving you forever changed.

DAY 6: SMALL ACTS, BIG LOVE

SETTING THE TABLE

Our days are busy and it can be hard to find time to quiet ourselves and be with God. Take some time to settle yourself. Find a comfortable place to sit. Breathe in . . . breathe out. Do that again. Breathe in . . . breathe out. Close your eyes and remember that God loves you!

This is our first week of Advent, the season of days before Christmas. We are waiting for the birth of Jesus! As we wait, we think about the many ways God is with us in our waiting. This is the week of hope. So this week, we are considering the ways that God's hope is showing up in the world around us.

No act of kindness, no matter
how small, is ever wasted.
— AESOP[8]

MATTHEW 4:18-20

As Jesus was walking beside the Sea of Galilee, he saw two brothers, Simon called Peter and his brother Andrew. They were casting a net into the lake, for they were fishermen. "Come, follow me," Jesus said, "and I will send you out to fish for people." At once they left their nets and followed him.

FOOD FOR THOUGHT

We learn a lot about ourselves because of our relationships and friendships with those around us. We learn that we can be funny when we make someone laugh. We know we are loved and lovable when we are wrapped in a hug or when our smiles are met by the warm smiles of our parents, grandparents, teachers, or friends. We discover we are smart, strong, brave, and trustworthy in the care of those who give us opportunities to try, to fail, to be held, and then to try again.

When I was a child, I had the gift of seeing myself through the eyes of my grandma. I knew I was loved because she told me every time she had the chance. When I entered her home, she would greet me with a "Yoo-hoo! I'm in here" as if she'd been expecting me, and I knew I was important. I knew she cared deeply about who I was becoming because she made it a point to handwrite letters asking about my life and interests. I knew I was smart and strong and brave because she had instilled that in me by giving me opportunities to try and try again, held in encouraging love.

My grandmother loved me BIG, but she didn't do it with big dramatic gestures. She did it with countless small acts of love that gave me a deep sense of importance and belonging.

Jesus also loved people BIG. When Jesus met people who were hungry, he fed them. When Jesus met people who felt lost, he invited them to eat with him. When Jesus met the disciples, he learned their names and invited them to be part of what he was doing. The way Jesus loved people gave them a deep sense of importance and belonging.

In this Advent season, let us remember together that one way we can carry hope into the world is to love people BIG through small acts of love that make others feel important.

BLESSiNG

God of Hope,
Help us to show BIG love to others
through small acts of love that
make a big difference.
Amen.

KiDS TABLE TALK

- Think of someone in your life who has made you feel especially loved. What was it about that person that was so special?

- Talk together about the ways that one small act can make a big difference—a ripple in a pond, a wave on the sand, the way a river of water can shape a mountain.

- It is easy to think that our everyday acts of kindness don't matter. Draw a heart on a piece of paper and keep it somewhere today that is visible to you. We never actually know how big a difference our small acts might make in the life of another. Today, try to notice the way that you can choose small acts of kindness towards others—and try to be especially aware of the ways that the acts of others bring love and hope to your own life.

DAY 7: EMBODY LOVE

SETTiNG THE TABLE

Our days are busy and it can be hard to find time to quiet ourselves and be with God. Take some time to settle yourself. Find a comfortable place to sit. Breathe in . . . breathe out. Do that again. Breathe in . . . breathe out. Close your eyes and remember that God loves you!

This is our first week of Advent, the season of days before Christmas. We are waiting for the birth of Jesus! As we wait, we think about the many ways God is with us in our waiting. This is the week of hope. So this week, we are considering the ways that God's hope is showing up in the world around us

And what happened then . . . ?
Well . . . in Who-ville they say
That the Grinch's small heart
Grew three sizes that day.
— DR. SEUSS[9]

JOHN 1:4
In him was life, and the life was the light of all people.

F⦿⦿D F⦿R TH⦿UGHT

One of my favorite Christmas movies is How the Grinch Stole Christmas. Maybe you like this movie, too? The Grinch is so annoyed by the joy of Christmas that he does all he can to ruin Christmas for everyone else. On Christmas Eve, he dresses up like Santa and sneaks into the village of Whoville to steal all the Christmas he can possibly fit on his sleigh.

The Grinch is sure that this will stop the Whos from celebrating on Christmas morning. But then the people of Whoville celebrate Christmas anyway—without the presents and trees, or the tinsel and feast that the Grinch took from them while they were sleeping. The Grinch is confused, and he wonders how Christmas came anyway:

"It came without ribbons, it came without tags.
It came without packages, boxes, or bags.
Maybe Christmas, he thought, doesn't come from a store.
Maybe Christmas, perhaps, means a little bit more."

The Grinch is right! Christmas means much, much more!

Even if there were no presents, no trees, no lights, or even Christmas songs on the radio, Christmas would still come, because the hope of Christmas is not found in things—it is found in love. The love of people who decorate their church during a war to bring joy; the love of someone who plants trees to protect their village; the love of a grandmother who makes gifts to show a grandchild she cares; the love found in kind, encouraging words; the love Mary has for her tiny baby who brings hope to our world.

Love is the spark that makes hope possible. Jesus is God's love and hope born into the world.

You are also God's love and hope born into the world. As you continue in this Advent journey, don't forget that the love you share is another way of bringing God's hope into the world.

BLESSiNG

God of Hope,
Help us never to lose our faith in the transformative power of love.
May we always be looking for the unexpected ways God's love is shining through us and bringing hope to those around us.
Amen.

KiDS TABLE TALK

- Think about or talk about the ways that you have shared love with those around you this week.

- How do small acts of love and kindness help you to see God's love? How do they help you to have hope for our world?

- Look back to that tiny light you placed in your window. How has this light been a reminder of hope for you? Pass this light on to someone you think might need it and explain how this symbol of light can be a reminder of God's love and hope in this season of Advent.

A WEEK OF PEACE

DAY 1: A SIMPLE KIND OF PEACE

SETTiNG THE TABLE

Welcome! You are welcome to come into this time of reflection JUST AS YOU ARE! Find a place that is most comfortable to you. If there are things bothering you right now, try letting them go for the next little bit. Take a deep breath and breathe in God's love for you. As you let that breath go, remember that God is with you in this moment.

This is our second week of Advent. We are still waiting for the birth of Jesus! As we continue to wait, we think about the many ways God is with us in our waiting. This is the week of peace. This week, we are considering the ways that God's peace is showing up in the world around us.

Imagine all the people
Living life in peace. . .
— JOHN LENNON[10]

ISAIAH 9:6
His name will be called Wonderful, Counselor, Mighty God, Everlasting Father, Prince of Peace.

FOOD FOR THOUGHT

Do you enjoy a good story? Do you enjoy sharing and listening to the stories of your friends?

I know I do!

My grandmother was a great storyteller. Every Sunday at lunch, we would all gather around the table as she shared stories of her childhood. We would hang on her every word. The way she would change her voice with each character—even the dog—filled the room with laughter and togetherness. She had a way of drawing people in with her humor and her love.

She taught us a lot of valuable lessons through those stories, and one of those lessons is that we can learn a lot about one another through the stories we share. In the experiences of others, we are given a gift of seeing the world around us through a different lens—like looking through a kaleidoscope.

The Bible is filled with stories that help us see and understand the love of God in new and beautiful ways.

In the story of Isaiah, the people felt lost and afraid, and were looking for help. Isaiah reminds them of a promise of peace yet to come. They were reminded that even when things feel scary, peace can show up for us and comfort our hearts.

One surprising thing we learn about peace through the story of God's love is that peace doesn't have to arrive in big ways. Sometimes peace can enter the world in small ways. Jesus brought the promise of peace into the world, even as a tiny baby.

From the moment Jesus was born, his parents and those who gathered around to celebrate his birth were filled with wonder, love, and a sense of peace. The story of Jesus's birth helps us see peace in a new way. It reminds us that part of God's love for us is the promise of a peace that—even when things are difficult or scary—is meant for us, for you and for me.

Peace is a gift that can be given in small ways. It is a gift and a promise we can offer to one another.

BLESSiNG

God of Peace,
Help us to see peace in the small moments.
Help us look for ways that we can share love and be bringers of peace in this world.
Amen.

KiDS TABLE TALK

- Share your favorite story with a friend or family member. What about that story makes it special?

- What does peace look like to you? What brings you peace?

- Remember that peace can be found in the simple, small gestures that we share with one another. Draw a picture of one way you can share peace with those around you (for example: a smile, saying a kind word, opening a door for someone else).

DAY 2: PEACE IN THE STORM

SETTING THE TABLE

Welcome! You are welcome to come into this time of reflection JUST AS YOU ARE! Find a place that is most comfortable to you. If there are things bothering you right now, try letting them go for the next little bit. Take a deep breath and breathe in God's love for you. As you let that breath go, remember that God is with you in this moment.

This is our second week of Advent. We are still waiting for the birth of Jesus! As we continue to wait, we think about the many ways God is with us in our waiting. This is the week of peace. This week, we are considering the ways that God's peace is showing up in the world around us.

Every storm runs out of rain.
— GARY ALLAN[11]

MARK 4:39
Jesus got up, rebuked the wind and said to the waves, "Quiet! Be still!" Then the wind died down and it was completely calm.

FOOD FOR THOUGHT

Storms can be really scary—there is loud thunder, bright lightning, and hard rain. . . . It can all feel big and frightening!

There are some things we experience in life that can also feel like an overwhelming storm: moving to a new school, a lot of worries, a lot of homework, or even changes at home.

Jesus's friends also felt afraid and overwhelmed sometimes. There is one story where they were in a boat during a raging storm with big waves that were breaking their ship into pieces. It felt like their boat was going to sink. They felt alone and hopeless, and cried out for help. Jesus answered their call. He calmed the waves, brought peace to the storm, and assured them that they were not alone.

Jesus was with them.

In the storms of life, we are not alone either. God is always with us—and we are surrounded by people who answer our cries and offer calm and peace in moments when we feel overwhelmed. We were never intended to do life on our own. We are created to be in community together, to watch out for one another and reach out, to offer moments of peace and comfort to one another—to be with each other in times of need.

Take time to notice how you are feeling each day. Some days, we might need to lean on the presence and attention of our friends and family. Other days, we might find that it is our turn to be a resting place, to provide a moment of peace for our friends and others we meet along the way.

BLESSING

God of Peace,

Life can sometimes feel like an overwhelming storm.

We are so thankful that you are with us to offer peace and rest.

We also give thanks for those in our world that answer our cries for help, and that remind us that we are not alone.

Help us to offer moments of peace in someone else's storm.

Amen.

KIDS TABLE TALK

- What brings you peace in a storm? What makes you feel better when you are feeling overwhelmed or anxious, worried or afraid?

- How can you remind others they are not alone?

- Peace can come in all shapes and sizes. How have you experienced peace? Draw a picture of something that gives you peace; share the picture with a friend.

DAY 3: A LITTLE PEACE AND QUIET

SETTING THE TABLE

Welcome! You are welcome to come into this time of reflection JUST AS YOU ARE! Find a place that is most comfortable to you. If there are things bothering you right now, try letting them go for the next little bit. Take a deep breath and breathe in God's love for you. As you let that breath go, remember that God is with you in this moment.

This is our second week of Advent. We are still waiting for the birth of Jesus! As we continue to wait, we think about the many ways God is with us in our waiting. This is the week of peace. This week, we are considering the ways that God's peace is showing up in the world around us.

In the stillness is where peace abounds.
— **OPRAH WINFREY**[12]

PSALM 46:10
Be still and know that I am God.

FOOD FOR THOUGHT

Has anyone ever asked you for "a little peace and quiet?"

Growing up, my younger sister and I would spend a week most summers with our grandparents in Buies Creek, NC. Every day, we couldn't wait until after lunch when we made our daily trip to the pool. But without fail, my grandmother would insist that we take a nap before we could go. I thought surely she would forget at least once, but no such luck. She insisted that we needed rest, "a little peace and quiet."

It can be hard to slow down if you're having fun, but the truth is that everyone needs to rest and reset. From babies to grandmas, it is essential for our minds, bodies, and souls.

Moments of quiet are like a "reset button." They allow us more patience and understanding with ourselves and one another.

Even Jesus needed these moments of stillness. Sometimes, when he was in a large crowd, he would go off to a quiet place to slow down, to focus and reconnect with God in prayer.

We need those moments as much as Jesus did.

We need to take time away from the busyness of life to listen to our feelings and our bodies, to refresh our hearts and our minds, and to give ourselves the capacity to have grace and patience with one another.

The psalmist hears God saying "Be still and know that I am God." In the coming days, we will sing "Silent night, holy night!/ All is calm, all is bright." Listen to these words and remember to find moments to be silent and still. Remember that God is with you in the small, quiet moments that bring you peace.

BLESSiNG

God of Peace,
Help us find moments of stillness
so that we can experience the fullness of who you are.
Amen.

KiDS TABLE TALK

- Draw a picture of your favorite way to relax. Is it reading a book? A trip to the beach? Nap time?

- Take a few moments to be still and quiet. What noises do you notice that you did not notice before (the birds singing, the wind blowing, friends laughing)?

- When you start to feel overwhelmed, try repeating the words of this blessing from the Psalms to calm your soul. Imagine God sharing them with you: "Be still and know that I am God."

DAY 4: FINDING PEACE IN FORGIVENESS

SETTING THE TABLE

Welcome! You are welcome to come into this time of reflection JUST AS YOU ARE! Find a place that is most comfortable to you. If there are things bothering you right now, try letting them go for the next little bit. Take a deep breath and breathe in God's love for you. As you let that breath go, remember that God is with you in this moment.

This is our second week of Advent. We are still waiting for the birth of Jesus! As we continue to wait, we think about the many ways God is with us in our waiting. This is the week of peace. This week, we are considering the ways that God's peace is showing up in the world around us.

It's one of the greatest gifts you can give yourself, to forgive. Forgive everybody.
— **MAYA ANGELOU**[13]

MATTHEW 18:21-22

Then Peter came up and said to him, "Lord, how often will my brother sin against me, and I forgive him? As many as seven times?" Jesus said to him, "I do not say to you seven times, but seventy-seven times."

FOOD FOR THOUGHT

Have you had your feelings hurt before? Have you hurt someone else's feelings?

It can be hard to say "I'm sorry" when we hurt others. It can also be difficult to accept apologies from our friends when they have said or done something hurtful to us.

There are some hurtful words and hurtful actions that can cause hurt for a long time. Carrying that hurt around isn't easy. It can feel really heavy, like you're carrying a big rock. Sometimes carrying big, heavy things can make us feel grumpy or angry. Sometimes we get tired and feel sad.

Jesus knew that sometimes it is better to put the rock down than carry it around all the time. Sometimes, it is better to let go of the hurt instead of holding it in our hearts. Jesus may have been sad and maybe even angry when his friends caused his heart to hurt—but instead of carrying that big hurt inside his heart, he offered a prayer: "Father, forgive them, for they know not what they do" (Luke 23:34). The prayer brought peace to his heart.

This wasn't just an idea that Jesus taught, it was an action that Jesus lived.

Forgiveness is not simply for the other person, it is for us too. Forgiveness allowed Jesus to find peace. It allowed him to let go of the hurt he felt instead of carrying it around.

Forgiveness gives our hearts space to heal. It allows our hearts to let go of those things that are heavy to carry so that we can fill up with joy and peace—which are easy to carry—in order to fully love ourselves and one another with all of our hearts.

BLESSING

God of Peace,
Give us the courage to forgive like you do,
so that we can have peace in our hearts.
Amen.

KIDS TABLE TALK

- Have you had your feelings hurt before? How did that make you feel?
- What was it like to offer forgiveness to the person? Was it hard? Did it make you feel better?
- How does offering forgiveness to others give you peace and offer peace to those around you?
- Create a comic of two friends after a disagreement. What does forgiveness look like? What words might we use to offer or ask for forgiveness?

DAY 5: OFFERING PEACE TO OUR NEIGHBORS

SETTING THE TABLE

Welcome! You are welcome to come into this time of reflection JUST AS YOU ARE! Find a place that is most comfortable to you. If there are things bothering you right now, try letting them go for the next little bit. Take a deep breath and breathe in God's love for you. As you let that breath go, remember that God is with you in this moment.

This is our second week of Advent. We are still waiting for the birth of Jesus! As we continue to wait, we think about the many ways God is with us in our waiting. This is the week of peace. This week, we are considering the ways that God's peace is showing up in the world around us.

Remember, what is given from the heart reaches the heart.
— **PATRICIA C. MCKISSACK**[14]

LUKE 10:29-37
Jesus asked, "Which of these three do you think was a neighbor to the man who fell into the hands of robbers?" The man replied, "The one who had mercy on him." Jesus told him, "Go and do likewise."

FOOD FOR THOUGHT

What does it really mean to love your neighbor?

Jesus tells a story of a man who is badly hurt and in need of help. In the story, two people walk by the man without stopping to help. Then, a third passerby sees the man and decides to help him. He kneels down beside him, cares for his wounds, and moves him to safety. His act of love offers peace to this stranger in need. When Jesus finishes telling this story, he asks "which of these three was the neighbor?" In other words, which one showed love and care for the man in need? Those listening to the story replied that the one who helped the man in need was the neighborly character in the story. The one who offered peace and comfort was the neighbor.

He does what we should all do: love our neighbor as best we can without exception. We are called to extend a hand in love regardless of our differences or our fears—and without condition.

When we help others, we offer a little bit of peace to them. We remind them that they are not alone and that someone cares.

With this story, Jesus reminds us to pay close attention to the needs of those around us, and to offer help to one another in ways that bring peace.

BLESSING

God of Peace,
Help us to love others.
Help us to view our neighbors through your eyes.
Help us to offer understanding, kindness, and peace.
Amen.

KIDS TABLE TALK

- Who are your neighbors? What does it mean to love your neighbor, and what does that look like in action?

- Try making a new friend. Offering a kind smile can go a long way toward building welcome in the world around you.

- Make a list of ways you can offer love and peace to your neighbor.

DAY 6: PEACE IN THE UNKNOWN

SETTiNG THE TABLE

Welcome! You are welcome to come into this time of reflection JUST AS YOU ARE! Find a place that is most comfortable to you. If there are things bothering you right now, try letting them go for the next little bit. Take a deep breath and breathe in God's love for you. As you let that breath go, remember that God is with you in this moment.

This is our second week of Advent. We are still waiting for the birth of Jesus! As we continue to wait, we think about the many ways God is with us in our waiting. This is the week of peace. This week, we are considering the ways that God's peace is showing up in the world around us.

Don't you know there's part of me that longs to go
Into the unknown?
— ELSA, FROZEN II[15]

MATTHEW 14:28-29

"Lord, if it's you," Peter replied, "tell me to come to you on the water." "Come," he said. Then Peter got down out of the boat, walked on the water and came toward Jesus.

FOOD FOR THOUGHT

A few Christmases ago I went with my family to see the Disney movie, Frozen II. It is one of my favorites!

Without giving away too much, it is a beautiful story of two sisters stepping into the unknown to follow a calling. In Elsa's case, it was an audible calling that only she could hear. Elsa is nervous, but she is not alone. She is with the person who knows her best: her sister, Anna. While Elsa's journey is the main storyline, Anna is also on a path to discovering her own calling. The two sisters depend on one another, they challenge one another, they encourage one another, and ultimately neither one can make the journey without the other.

Have you ever felt a little nervous in a new situation? How did it make you feel to see a familiar face or to receive encouragement from a friend in those moments?

The unknown can be a scary place, but the love and encouragement from friends can give us comfort.

It makes me think about the story of Peter, when Jesus calls him out onto the water. He is doing it! Taking it one step at a time, he is walking on the water! But when Peter becomes afraid, he starts to sink. The fear of what might happen in this new situation makes Peter nervous, and he cries out for help. Jesus reaches out his hand and catches him.

Jesus did not leave Peter to navigate the waters alone. Jesus encourages Peter because he knows he can do it. He was doing it, he just had to keep going. Peter finds peace in the support and encouragement of a friend—in Jesus.

We are supposed to do the same thing for each other. When there is no map for the journey, we can step in and offer each other love and encouragement to keep moving forward. We can reach out a hand and walk with someone through uncertainty, fear, and doubt. We can walk beside one another and challenge each other to do our best.

We can give our support and encouragement, offering a little more peace to one another in this world of unknowns and new opportunities.

BLESSiNG

God of Peace,
The unknown can be scary and lonely.
Help us to reach out to one another with an open heart of love,
and to offer support and peace through the gift of encouraging words.
Amen.

KiDS TABLE TALK

- Have you ever felt lost? What did that feel like? What made you feel better?

- Has there ever been a new kid in your class? Were you ever the new kid? How does it feel when a new friend asks you to play?

- What does it mean to encourage someone? Make a list of ways that you can be a person who encourages others.

DAY 7: DREAMERS OF PEACE

SETTiNG THE TABLE

Welcome! You are welcome to come into this time of reflection JUST AS YOU ARE! Find a place that is most comfortable to you. If there are things bothering you right now, try letting them go for the next little bit. Take a deep breath and breathe in God's love for you. As you let that breath go, remember that God is with you in this moment.

This is our second week of Advent. We are still waiting for the birth of Jesus! As we continue to wait, we think about the many ways God is with us in our waiting. This is the week of peace. This week, we are considering the ways that God's peace is showing up in the world around us.

Imagine what you could do.
— **JUAN FELIPE HERRERA**[16]

You may say I'm a dreamer
But I'm not the only one
I hope someday you'll join us
And the world will live as one
— JOHN LENNON[17]

JOHN 14:27
"Peace I leave with you; my peace I give you. I do not give to you as the world gives. Do not let your hearts be troubled and do not be afraid."

FOOD FOR THOUGHT

Are you a dreamer? What do you dream about? Do you daydream about your future?

Jesus was a dreamer.

Little by little, he transformed the way people saw God and the way they saw one another. Jesus said that all the rules and the laws could be this simple: "Love God and love one another."

Jesus knew that the world wasn't always so simple, but it was the dream Jesus had for the world, and he believed it was possible. Jesus was showing us the way to have peace on earth, and he challenged all of us to be a part of it—to love each other the way God loves each of us.

Can you imagine a world where everyone loves each other? How wonderful that would be!

There would be no conflict and we would all get along. It may seem hard to achieve, but we can work together toward love even when it seems hard.

It may not be the way that the world is now, but it is the dream in our hearts that we believe is possible. And we must continue to dream.

If we truly believe there can be peace on earth, we have to first dream it. That dream starts with you and with me.

BLESSiNG

God of Peace,
You gave us the greatest gift, which was the gift of love.
Help us to share your love more freely,
and to spread peace on earth.
Amen.

KiDS TABLE TALK

- What does it mean to love each other unconditionally? This is the way God loves each of us.

- It's through our love that we are able to be the peace on earth that we dream of. How do we express our love for others in the world?

- Draw a picture of what love looks like to you.

A WEEK OF JOY

DAY 1: JOY TO THE WORLD, THE LORD HAS COME

SETTING THE TABLE

This is a time during your day when you can simply be. Take a moment to settle in. Place one hand on your heart and your other hand on your belly. Breathe in deeply . . . and then let it go. Do this five more times. With each breath, think of something in your life that you are thankful for.

This is our third week of Advent, those days that come before Christmas. As we continue to wait for baby Jesus to be born, we think together about the many ways God is with us in our waiting. This is the week of joy. This week, we are considering the ways that God's joy is showing up in our families, our communities, and our world.

Joy to the world, the Lord has come! Let Earth receive her King!
— TRADITIONAL CHRISTMAS HYMN

PSALMS 98:4
Let the whole earth shout to the Lord; be jubilant, shout for joy, and sing.

FOoD FoR THOUGHT

"Joy to the world! The Lord has come! Let earth receive her king!"

Have you heard this song before? Do you know what it's about? It's a song about the good news of Jesus' birth. It's telling us to be joyful—to be deeply glad and grateful—because the one who shows us God's love for the world, the one who shows us how to live our lives with God and each other, has finally been born into the world. How exciting is that?!

When Jesus was born, the world was filled with joy and celebration—and not just from the people you might expect. Of course, his parents were excited that he was born, but so were the animals who shared their hay so Jesus could have a bed, and the angels who sang loud songs from the heavens, and the shepherds who ran in from the fields just to see his cute feet and face. Everyone had been waiting a long time for this special baby to enter the world—and when he did, the world erupted with joy!

Waiting can be really hard, but there is a lot of joy that comes when the waiting ends and what we are waiting for finally arrives.

Christmas is just around the corner, and I bet you can hardly contain your excitement! It probably feels like Christmas could not come any slower! But it will come eventually, it always does. And when the waiting is finally over, we also will erupt with joy!

This week, as you wait, try not to get impatient in your waiting. Instead, try to look for joy in your excitement about what is coming. Look for joy in remembering that our Christmas story is the story of God's love for the world. Look for joy when you see a baby and remember that at one time

Jesus was that little too. And look for joy when you sing those familiar Christmas carols that tell of the good news of this tiny baby Jesus. Joy to the World! The Lord has come!

BLESSING

God of Joy,
Thank you for loving us.
Thank you for the ways joy fills our world
during this season.
Help us spread that joy to those around us, even when it's hard.
Amen.

KIDS TABLE TALK

- What are some of your favorite Christmas carols? Why do you like those the most?
- How have you experienced moments of joy this week?
- How have you shared joy with others this week?

DAY 2: FAITH LIKE HANNAH

SETTiNG THE TABLE

This is a time during your day when you can simply be. Take a moment to settle in. Place one hand on your heart and your other hand on your belly. Breathe in deeply . . . and then let it go. Do this five more times. With each breath, think of something in your life that you are thankful for.

This is our third week of Advent, those days that come before Christmas. As we continue to wait for baby Jesus to be born, we think together about the many ways God is with us in our waiting. This is the week of joy. This week, we are considering the ways that God's joy is showing up in our families, our communities, and our world.

My heart is a window, my heart is a slide. My heart can be closed or opened up wide. Some days it's a puddle. Some days it's a stain. Some days it is cloudy and heavy with rain. . . . There are days it is broken, but broken can mend, and a heart that is closed can still open again.
— **CORINNA LUYKEN**[18]

1 SAMUEL 2:1
My heart rejoices in the LORD; in the LORD my horn is lifted high.

F**O**oD F**o**R TH**O**UGHT

It can be hard to say goodbye to people we love—especially if we know it might be a long time before we see them again.

When the school year closes for summer break, we dread the months we will spend away from friends we are used to seeing every day in the classroom. When summer camp comes to an end, it makes us sad when those new friends we've made have to return to their own homes. When a friend moves away, it is really hard to imagine how our lives will change without that person close by to talk to or play with. Saying goodbye is hard!

This reminds me of one of my favorite stories in the Bible, the story of Hannah. After waiting and praying for a child for a long time, Hannah had a son named Samuel. Hannah loved Samuel so very much! She loved being his mother and watching him grow, and she enjoyed being an important part of his life.

But even though she loved her son, when Samuel was old enough, Hannah brought him to serve God in the temple. This was a commitment that meant Samuel would live at the temple instead of at home with her.

This had to be really hard for Hannah. I bet it even made her pretty sad. But even so, the story says that she lifted up praises to God. Hannah says, "My heart rejoices in the LORD; in the LORD my horn is lifted high."

Even though it was hard for Hannah to be apart from Samuel, Hannah found joy in her deep love for him and in knowing that Samuel was doing something important for God.

76

There will be times in your life when you'll have to say goodbye for a while. Goodbyes can be difficult, but usually when they are hard it is because there is so much goodness to celebrate about the people we will miss. And so, in our moments of goodbyes, we can offer gratitude and joy for the ones we love. We can give thanks for the love they've shared. And we can delight in the joy they have given us that we carry in our hearts until we meet again.

BLESSiNG

God of Joy,
Help us to have faith like Hannah—
to find peace even in uncertain times,
and to find joy even during hard goodbyes.
Amen.

KiDS TABLE TALK

- Have you ever had to tell someone goodbye? How did that make you feel?

- Draw or paint a picture of your goodbye. If you have seen them again, draw or paint a picture of your reunion. If you have not seen them yet, draw or paint three things you would like to share with them when you get to see them again. Give thanks for the things you hope to share one day.

- Hang that picture on your refrigerator or on your wall as a reminder of all the ways that person brings joy to your life.

DAY 3: FINDING JOY WHEN YOU FEEL SAD

SETTING THE TABLE

This is a time during your day when you can simply be. Take a moment to settle in. Place one hand on your heart and your other hand on your belly. Breathe in deeply . . . and then let it go. Do this five more times. With each breath, think of something in your life that you are thankful for.

This is our third week of Advent, those days that come before Christmas. As we continue to wait for baby Jesus to be born, we think together about the many ways God is with us in our waiting. This is the week of joy. This week, we are considering the ways that God's joy is showing up in our families, our communities, and our world.

Always keep a little prayer in your pocket,
and you're sure to see the light;
soon there'll be joy and happiness,
and your little world will be bright.
— "SOMEONE'S WAITING FOR YOU"[19]

HABAKKUK 3:18

"Yet I will rejoice in the Lord, I will be joyful in God my savior."

FOOD FOR THOUGHT

Have you ever worked really hard to create something and without warning it completely fell apart?

Maybe you were building the most beautiful sandcastle, and the tide came in and washed it away. Maybe you were building the tallest Lego tower or a really incredible fort, and your little brother or sister brought it down with a crash!

How did that make you feel? Were you disappointed? Was it hard for you to imagine where to rebuild? Where do you begin?

There are a lot of people who understand the way that feels.

In the Bible, there is a story about a prophet named Habakkuk. Habakkuk is struggling through his own feelings of disappointment and sadness because his home has been destroyed. The food and water for his community is in short supply, and he feels like there is nothing he can do to help. Can you imagine feeling this way?

Habakkuk—even when it seems like all hope should be lost—says that he will still be joyful in God! Even in his lowest moment, when he was trying to imagine where to begin rebuilding his home, Habakkuk remembers that God is with him and that God loves him—and that brings him joy.

We, too, are called to be there for one another. To be a helping hand and a source of God's joy in the midst of sadness and in disappointment.

Sadness is an emotion that we all feel sometimes. Sometimes something happens that makes you feel sad—like that sandcastle that the tide washed away; or that fort that came crashing down. Then, there might be other times that you really don't know why you are sad. You just are.

Sadness can be a hard emotion to figure out, but what Habakkuk shows us is that, even in our saddest moments, we are not alone. We can lean on the love of our friends and family, and we can always be sure that God is still with us, that God loves us, and that God takes great joy in us.

That is something worth celebrating!

BLESSING

God of Joy,
Give us patience when we feel like giving up.
Give us strength to lean on those around us when we need it.
And help us to find joy in knowing that you are with us all the time.
Amen.

KIDS TABLE TALK

- Draw a picture of what it feels like to be sad or scared.

- What are some things you can do to make yourself feel better when you're sad? Listen to your favorite song, do jumping jacks, talk to someone, or simply cry?

- What are ways you can make someone else feel better who is sad? Give them a hug, write them a kind note, or listen to what's bothering them?

DAY 4: A JOYFUL HOMECOMING

SETTING THE TABLE

This is a time during your day when you can simply be. Take a moment to settle in. Place one hand on your heart and your other hand on your belly. Breathe in deeply . . . and then let it go. Do this five more times. With each breath, think of something in your life that you are thankful for.

This is our third week of Advent, those days that come before Christmas. As we continue to wait for baby Jesus to be born, we think together about the many ways God is with us in our waiting. This is the week of joy. This week, we are considering the ways that God's joy is showing up in our families, our communities, and our world.

There's no place like home.
— DOROTHY, THE WIZARD OF OZ[20]

ISAIAH 35:10
And those the LORD has rescued will return. . . . Gladness and joy will overtake them, and sorrow and sighing will flee away.

FOOD FOR THOUGHT

Have you ever been homesick?

That can be a terrible feeling! Maybe you were away at a friend's house or at camp, and it felt like you had been gone FOREVER! You couldn't wait to see your family, friends, or pets again, could you?

Do you remember the day you finally got to go back home?! Do you remember that first big hug from somebody you loved and had missed so much?!

There is a joy that overcomes us when we are reunited with people we love. We feel more at home, we feel safer, we feel more comfortable and able to be ourselves—and that brings us joy!

That's what Isaiah 35 reminds me of. This chapter beautifully tells us of God's people returning home, singing and completely overtaken by gladness and everlasting joy. How wonderful that we have a home in God, a place we can completely be ourselves.

With God, there's no need for any pretending. We can show up as we truly are and be embraced with loving acceptance.

BLESSING

God of Joy,
Thank you for loving us more than we can ever imagine.
Thank you for offering us a place of rest and comfort
where we can feel wholly accepted.
Amen.

KIDS TABLE TALK

- Who can you completely be yourself around?

- Is there any time that you feel like you have to hide part of your personality? Why do you feel this way?

- It's awesome to have people in our lives who let us completely be ourselves! The next time you're with the person you feel you can be yourself around, let them know how special they are to you.

DAY 5: BE NOT AFRAID

SETTING THE TABLE

This is a time during your day when you can simply be. Take a moment to settle in. Place one hand on your heart and your other hand on your belly. Breathe in deeply . . . and then let it go. Do this five more times. With each breath, think of something in your life that you are thankful for.

This is our third week of Advent, those days that come before Christmas. As we continue to wait for baby Jesus to be born, we think together about the many ways God is with us in our waiting. This is the week of joy. This week, we are considering the ways that God's joy is showing up in our families, our communities, and our world.

It's okay to be scared. Being scared means you're about to do something really, really brave.
— MANDY HALE[21]

ISAIAH 41:10
So do not fear, for I am with you.

FOOD FOR THOUGHT

Let's talk about fear for a second!

Fear can certainly be a good thing! It keeps us safe by letting us know that something could be dangerous. But sometimes fear can also keep us from doing really cool things like meeting new people, trying new foods, auditioning for a play, or trying out for a sport.

It's totally normal to be scared to do something new. I think we get scared because when we try new things, we might mess up and feel silly. But it's okay to mess up, and it's okay to feel silly. God didn't make us perfect. God just made us . . . US! And God made each of us very special.

Never before and never again will there EVER be another you. How crazy is that?! That means no one before or after you can give this world what you have the potential to give it. You have a light inside of you. Let it shine big and bright! God may call you to do something new one day, a cool new thing that only you can do like you can do it! If you feel scared, just remember that God has promised to be with you. You might feel afraid, but don't let that stop you.

God says, "Do not fear, for I am with you. . . . Do not fear, . . . I have called you by name" (Isaiah 41:10; 43:1). God loves you, God cares for you, and God made you to be just as you are—and this God who loves you, calls you by your name to do big, important things in the world.

Give a big, joyful shout for the wonderfully, fearlessly, uniquely made YOU!

BLESSING

God of Joy,
Help us let go of our fears so that we can do
the cool new things you have in store for us!
Help us to know that it's okay to mess up
because you will love us and be with us no matter what.

KIDS TABLE TALK

- Have you ever done something new? How did that make you feel—were you excited or nervous? Were you calm?

- Is there something new that you would like to try?

- How does it make you feel to know that you are uniquely made—that never before and never again will there ever be another you? Be sure to share the joyful news with someone else this week that they are wonderfully made and amazing just as they are!

DAY 6: JOY, FOR SUCH A TIME AS THIS

SETTïNG THE TABLE

This is a time during your day when you can simply be. Take a moment to settle in. Place one hand on your heart and your other hand on your belly. Breathe in deeply . . . and then let it go. Do this five more times. With each breath, think of something in your life that you are thankful for.

This is our third week of Advent, those days that come before Christmas. As we continue to wait for baby Jesus to be born, we think together about the many ways God is with us in our waiting. This is the week of joy. This week, we are considering the ways that God's joy is showing up in our families, our communities, and our world.

There is freedom waiting for you
On the breezes of the sky
And you ask, "What if I fall?"
Oh, but my darling
What if you fly?
— ERIN HANSON[22]

ESTHER 4:14
And who knows but that you have come to your royal position for such a time as this?

FOOD FOR THOUGHT

What do you think it means to "make a difference"?

Take a minute to think about or name aloud some people in our world who have made a big difference. Here are a few to help you get started: Wangari Matthai, Malala Yousafzai, Martin Luther King Jr., Ruby Bridges. Can you think of some people in your own life who have made a big difference?

Do you think that you have the ability to make a difference?

Well, guess what? You DO!

The Bible holds many stories about how God uses all kinds of people, especially children, to make very important differences.

One time, a young boy named David defeated a giant bully when no one else could do it! Another time, a baby who was born into slavery grew up and led God's people to freedom. His name was Moses. Then there was Esther, a brave orphan girl who became a queen. As queen, she risked her own safety to save thousands of lives.

Sometimes it can be hard to believe that we have the strength, the courage, or the ability to make a difference. But joy and deliverance can come through any of us, as small or insignificant as we may feel. Don't underestimate the amazing things you can do!

BLESSiNG

God of Joy,
Thank you for giving us the power to make a difference in our world!
Teach us to love others as you have loved us.
Amen.

KiDS TABLE TALK

- Who is someone who has made a difference in your life?

- Sit down with some paper, crayons, and markers, and write a thank-you note to that person. Your kindness and gratitude may make a difference in their life too!

- What are some other ways that you can make a positive difference in your community?

DAY 7: MAKING SPACE FOR JOY

SETTING THE TABLE

This is a time during your day when you can simply be. Take a moment to settle in. Place one hand on your heart and your other hand on your belly. Breathe in deeply . . . and then let it go. Do this five more times. With each breath, think of something in your life that you are thankful for.

This is our third week of Advent, those days that come before Christmas. As we continue to wait for baby Jesus to be born, we think together about the many ways God is with us in our waiting. This is the week of joy. This week, we are considering the ways that God's joy is showing up in our families, our communities, and our world.

I've got the joy, joy, joy, joy, down in my heart!
— GEORGE W. COOKE[23]

NEHEMIAH 8:10
Do not grieve, for the joy of the LORD is your strength.

FOOD FOR THOUGHT

Have you ever been around someone who can't stop laughing and, even if you have no idea why they're laughing, suddenly you find yourself laughing, too?

That's because joy is contagious! When we experience joy, we invite those around us to experience joy too. How wonderful! There are many ways you can share joy with others. You can give a kind smile to a stranger; you can teach a friend how to do something you love to do; or you could give some encouragement to a classmate who might be struggling with a particular school subject.

Joy can even be found in times of pain. A lot of times, when we feel hurt inside we keep it all to ourselves—perhaps we feel embarrassed, or maybe we feel like no one will understand. But you never know— someone around you could have similar feelings, too, and you sharing your feelings could help them to feel better about sharing theirs. Imagine the joy both of you would feel having been able to share your feelings and knowing that you are not alone!

In our Bible verse today, Nehemiah invites those around him to celebrate with such joy that it spills over to those who cannot yet bring themselves to join in—those who may be struggling with sadness, anger, or feelings of pain. I believe God is inviting you, too, to share the joy you have inside so that love can spread the whole world wide!

BLESSING

God of Joy,

Thank you for your selfless, generous spirit.

Help us to see ways that we can spread joy in our communities and our world.

Amen.

KIDS TABLE TALK

- What brings you joy?

- Has there been a time when a friend made you feel better when you were hurting inside? What did they do to help you?

- What are some ways that you can share joy?

A WEEK OF LOVE

DAY 1: BETTER TOGETHER

SETTING THE TABLE

Find a quiet, comfortable place to sit and be. Look around you. What do you notice? Close your eyes. What do you hear? Take a moment to check in with yourself. What is something today that gave you joy? What is something today that frustrated you? Now try to just focus on what's happening right now. As you enter this time, know that you are deeply loved!

This is our final week of Advent! We are almost at the end of our waiting. Jesus is almost here, and we can feel ourselves getting more and more excited. As we continue in this final week of waiting, we remember that God is with us. This final week is the week of love. This week, we are considering the ways that God's love is showing up in little ways and surprising ways all the time!

I'm not meant to be like you;
you're not meant to be like me.
Sometimes we will get along,
and sometimes we will disagree.

I know that we don't look the same:
our skin, our eyes, our hair, our frame.
But that does not dictate our worth;
we both have places here on earth.
And in the end we are right here
to live a life of love, not fear . . .
— **GRACE BYERS**[24]

LUKE 1:26-28, 30-31

In the sixth month, the angel Gabriel was sent by God to a town in Galilee called Nazareth, to a young woman engaged to a man whose name was Joseph, of the House of David. The young woman's name was Mary. And he came to her and said, "Greetings favored one! The Lord is with you . . . Do not be afraid, Mary, for you have found favor with God. And now you will . . . bear a son, and you will name him Jesus."

FOOD FOR THOUGHT

There is such beautiful diversity among God's creation.

There are plants, trees and flowers, insects and spiders, creatures that live underground and those that fly through the sky. There are fish and animals that live in the oceans, rivers, and lakes. There are creatures that make homes in trees, that roam over the land, that rest in caves. There are high mountains and tiny pebbles, low valleys, rolling hills, and flat plains. There are stars and moons and planets and vast galaxies yet unexplored. And in each of those categories there is so much variation in color, texture, preferences, shape, purpose, and beauty. It's truly amazing!

People are like that, too. We were not created to be exactly the same as one another. We are different in our appearances and our likes and dislikes, in our thoughts and in our opinions. Sometimes we get along well with each other, and other times we disagree about things. But just because we are different and may disagree, it doesn't mean we can't also appreciate one another. We can try to find the good in each person. We can show kindness and love to others, even when we don't agree with them, and even when they may not be the kindest to us. We know that everyone has hard days sometimes. Maybe the little bit of love and goodness we offer to someone who is having a difficult time will be the gift they need to be a little bit kinder and more generous with their own love in the world.

Jesus believed that everyone was worthy of love and kindness. Jesus had disagreements with his friends sometimes, but he still made room for them at his table, took care of them, and told them that God loved them. He also reminded them that God's love was not just for them, but was meant to be shared. It is something that we can bear into the world through our kind words, in our helpfulness, in our apologies when we hurt someone's feelings, and in the ways that we seek opportunities for growth and learning in ourselves and one another.

We give thanks for the light and love born into the world through Jesus, and we give thanks for the light and love that will be born into the world through each beautiful child of God.

BLESSING

God of Love,
Our world is so fascinating!
Thank you for keeping things interesting.
The diversity we see is a reflection of your expansive creativity.
Help us to appreciate the differences in one another, and to meet each

other in the world with kindness, grace, and love.
Amen.

KiDS TABLE TALK

- Think about or talk about some of your favorite animals. How are they alike and different? What do you like about the animals you chose?

- Think about some of your own friends or siblings. In what ways are you different? What are some things that you share in common? What makes each of you special?

- Draw a picture of your favorite animals and your favorite people in the world. Be sure to include all the things that make you different as a way to remember that God has made us all unique and special.

DAY 2: YOU ARE NOT ALONE

SETTING THE TABLE

Find a quiet, comfortable place to sit and be. Look around you. What do you notice? Close your eyes. What do you hear? Take a moment to check in with yourself. What is something today that gave you joy? What is something today that frustrated you? Now try to just focus on what's happening right now. As you enter this time, know that you are deeply loved!

This is our final week of Advent! We are almost at the end of our waiting. Jesus is almost here, and we can feel ourselves getting more and more excited. As we continue in this final week of waiting, we remember that God is with us. This final week is the week of love. This week, we are considering the ways that God's love is showing up in little ways and surprising ways all the time!

Wherever you find charity and love, God is there too.
— "UBI CARITAS," TRADITIONAL HYMN

If you see someone without a smile, give 'em yours.
— DOLLY PARTON[25]

MATTHEW 1:23
"And they shall name him Emmanuel," which means, "God is with us."

FOOD FOR THOUGHT

Do you ever feel lonely?

There are certainly times when we find ourselves alone. Being alone can be a fine thing. Having time to yourself can be a peaceful time, a restful time, a quiet time. It can be a time when you can imagine or play just the way you like.

But being alone is different from feeling lonely.

When we feel lonely we often feel sad about being alone. We may feel as though we don't have any friends, or feel that we don't have anyone to share things with, or perhaps we are missing someone we love. Everyone feels lonely sometimes.

Some people called Jesus "Emmanuel," which means "God is with us." It was a fitting name for Jesus because the way Jesus cared for others helped them feel less lonely and reminded them that God loved them.

When we care for others, it reminds them that they matter to us and that they are loved; it takes some of the loneliness out of the world. It sure feels good to feel less lonely. It is a gift we can bring to one another in our loving and in our caring each day.

BLESSING

God of Love,

When we are feeling lonely, help us remember that we are never truly alone because you are with us. Help us to care for others in the world so that they know they are loved, and feel less lonely.

Amen.

KIDS TABLE TALK

- Can you think of a time when you felt lonely? What made you feel better?

- Sometimes we might notice that our friends at school seem lonely or sad. What can you say or do to make them feel better?

- Offer some caring and kind words of encouragement to someone who might be feeling lonely. You might say, "God loves you," or "I just want you to know that you matter in this world," or "You are a gift to the world," or in this season you can say, "Happy Holidays" or "Merry Christmas."

DAY 3: THE IMPORTANCE OF REST

SETTiNG THE TABLE

Find a quiet, comfortable place to sit and be. Look around you. What do you notice? Close your eyes. What do you hear? Take a moment to check in with yourself. What is something today that gave you joy? What is something today that frustrated you? Now try to just focus on what's happening right now. As you enter this time, know that you are deeply loved!

This is our final week of Advent! We are almost at the end of our waiting. Jesus is almost here, and we can feel ourselves getting more and more excited. As we continue in this final week of waiting, we remember that God is with us. This final week is the week of love. This week, we are considering the ways that God's love is showing up in little ways and surprising ways all the time!

It is easier to build strong children than to repair broken adults.
— **ANONYMOUS**

'Twas the night before Christmas, when all through the house
not a creature was stirring, not even a mouse.
— **CLEMENT C. MOORE**[26]

GENESIS 2:2
And on the seventh day God finished the work that he had done, and he
rested on the seventh day from all the work that he had done.

FOoD FoR THOUGHT

"Come here to me," my grandma used to say when I was little. In those
moments when I was feeling tired or a bit out of sorts, she would scoop
me up, put me on her lap, hold me in her arms, and rock me into rest.

Sometimes we need that invitation to rest! Our days are pretty busy
with school or daycare, with playing, with friends, with fun activities
like gymnastics or soccer, chess or piano. And while all those things are
wonderful and fun, we also need times that our bodies and our minds are
not so busy. We need rest.

Rest is important for our health and wellbeing. There are lots of ways
to rest: lying down in the grass to listen as the birds chirp, sitting on
a swing to feel the wind blow, closing our eyes to enjoy an afternoon
nap. Nap time is not always the most fun time, but it is the best way
to rest. Our bodies and minds heal themselves when we're resting and
sleeping. When we rest, energy is restored to our bodies so that we have
the strength, coordination, and clarity we need when we are awake and
working, playing, and learning.

When God created the world, it says that God spent the last day resting.
Even God rested! Resting is a part of loving ourselves, and when we

encourage others to take the rest they need, we are also showing love to them.

BLESSiNG

God of Love,
Remind me that rest is a good thing, and help me to embrace nap times and rest times eagerly, so that I can be the healthiest version of myself. Amen.

KiDS TABLE TALK

- What are some ways you enjoy resting your body?

- How can you make sure that you take time to rest every day?

- Try resting every day for a week and then check back in with yourself to see how resting makes you feel better or more energized.

DAY 4: WRAPPED IN LOVE

SETTING THE TABLE

Find a quiet, comfortable place to sit and be. Look around you. What do you notice? Close your eyes. What do you hear? Take a moment to check in with yourself. What is something today that gave you joy? What is something today that frustrated you? Now try to just focus on what's happening right now. As you enter this time, know that you are deeply loved!

This is our final week of Advent! We are almost at the end of our waiting. Jesus is almost here, and we can feel ourselves getting more and more excited. As we continue in this final week of waiting, we remember that God is with us. This final week is the week of love. This week, we are considering the ways that God's love is showing up in little ways and surprising ways all the time!

"When I grow up," I tell her, "I too will go to faraway places and come home to live by the sea."
"That is all very well, little Alice," says my aunt, "but there is a third thing you must do."

"What is that?" I ask.
"You must do something to make the world more beautiful."
— **BARBARA COONEY**[27]

COLOSSIANS 3:14
Above all, clothe yourselves with love, which binds everything together in perfect harmony.

1 JOHN 4:7
Beloved, let us love one another.

FOOD FOR THOUGHT

To bind something means to wrap it up, or to hold something together.

You might think of wrapping a present, for example. The ribbon and bow on presents were originally used to keep the wrapping from coming apart. Nowadays we use tape for that purpose and the bow is mostly decorative, although some folks do still hold things together with the ribbon itself.

You can also think of wrapping a baby in a blanket, or maybe you like to wrap yourself up in a blanket sometimes. Blankets can help us feel cozy and warm, and even provide a sense of comfort and security.

People use a needle and thread to sew things together—clothing, blankets, stuffed animals, and baby dolls. That is also a way of binding things together so that they don't lose their fluff or stuffing, so that they don't fall apart.

We can hold each other, and we can wrap each other up in love. Hugs are one way we can do this, but even at a distance we can surround one another with love. We can mail cards of encouragement, or send messages with kind words. We can draw pictures for each other of beautiful things that bring us joy. We can send gifts, and call each other, and let people know that we think they're special. Using kind words, being gentle with each other's feelings, letting people know you care about them—these are all ways of wrapping people up in love. It is one of the best and most beautiful gifts we can offer in our world.

God wraps us up in love. Every piece and person of God's beautiful creation matters and is worthy of love, and there is nowhere we can go where God's love does not surround us with care and compassion.

BLESSiNG
God of Love,
Help me surround others with love, and may I, also, feel wrapped up in love each day.
I pray that everyone knows they are worthy of love, and I pray my words and actions will allow them to see the special person they are in your eyes.
Amen.

KiDS TABLE TALK
- Think about or talk about things that make you feel comfortable, safe, and loved.

- Do you like hugs? Some people do and others do not. We respect each other and each other's space and bodies. If someone does not want a hug, what are some other ways you can show that you care?

- Ask someone to help you wrap a present in this season of giving. As you wrap the present, offer words of kindness to the recipient. You can say them out loud as you wrap, write them in a note for them to receive with the present, or say them quietly in your heart as you wrap, as a prayer for the other person.

DAY 5: WHAT TRULY MATTERS

SETTING THE TABLE

Find a quiet, comfortable place to sit and be. Look around you. What do you notice? Close your eyes. What do you hear? Take a moment to check in with yourself. What is something today that gave you joy? What is something today that frustrated you? Now try to just focus on what's happening right now. As you enter this time, know that you are deeply loved!

This is our final week of Advent! We are almost at the end of our waiting. Jesus is almost here, and we can feel ourselves getting more and more excited. As we continue in this final week of waiting, we remember that God is with us. This final week is the week of love. This week, we are considering the ways that God's love is showing up in little ways and surprising ways all the time!

For never before in story or rhyme
(not even once upon a time)
has the world ever known a you, my friend,
and it never will, not ever again . . .
— **NANCY TILLMAN**[28]

117

MARK 9:37
Whoever welcomes one of these little children in my name welcomes me.

F●●D F●R TH●UGHT

We will celebrate Christmas soon—Jesus's birthday! Are you ready to celebrate?

On the day you were born, you were welcomed into the world for the first time. You were celebrated by people who loved you, those near and far away. Though they had never met you before, they were so excited for your presence in the world, and for the hope and possibility of all that you are. You are a wonderful gift to the world, and so loved. You are worth celebrating!

Jesus's parents welcomed Jesus into the world when he was born. They made sure he had a place to sleep, and they took care of him and showed him love. They weren't the only ones—the angels and shepherds and some wise folks came and brought gifts. They celebrated Jesus, and were hopeful for all he would bring to the world: peace, kindness, gentleness, forgiveness, and love.

Jesus says that when we offer welcome and kindness to even the littlest among us, we are just like the ones who welcomed little Jesus into the world with joy. Jesus believed that we are all worthy of welcome and celebration. Our moments of welcome to one another are little moments of Christmas that we create all year long through simple acts of love toward one another. Isn't that a beautiful thought?

BLESSING

God of Love,
Help me welcome others and offer kindness to those around me in all I do.
Help me create little moments of Christmas all year long.
Amen.

KIDS TABLE TALK

- There are lots of ways we can offer welcome to those around us. Can you think of a few ways you can offer welcome to those around you?

- What does it mean to be kind? Has anyone shown kindness to you? How did that act of kindness make you feel?

- Can you think of someone who might need a kind act of welcome? With the help of an adult, make a gift—a bracelet, a card, some cookies—and give that gift sometime this week.

DAY 6: CHRISTMAS EVE: MAKING ROOM

SETTING THE TABLE

Find a quiet, comfortable place to sit and be. Look around you. What do you notice? Close your eyes. What do you hear? Take a moment to check in with yourself. What is something today that gave you joy? What is something today that frustrated you? Now try to just focus on what's happening right now. As you enter this time, know that you are deeply loved!

This is our final week of Advent! We are almost at the end of our waiting. Jesus is almost here, and we can feel ourselves getting more and more excited. As we continue in this final week of waiting, we remember that God is with us. This final week is the week of love. This week, we are considering the ways that God's love is showing up in little ways and surprising ways all the time!

And the table
will be wide.
And the welcome
will be wide.

And the arms
will open wide
to gather us in.
And our hearts
will be open wide
to receive.
— **JAN RICHARDSON**[29]

LUKE 2:8-12

Now in that same region there were shepherds living in the fields, keeping watch over their flock by night. Then an angel of the Lord stood before them, and the glory of the Lord shone around them, and they were terrified. But the angel said to them, "Do not be afraid, for see, I am bringing you good news of great joy for all the people: to you is born this day in the city of David a Savior, who is the Messiah, the Lord. This will be a sign for you: you will find a child wrapped in bands of cloth and lying in a manger."

FOOD FOR THOUGHT

Jesus's parents, Mary and Joseph, were traveling to Bethlehem when the time came for Jesus to be born. When they arrived in Bethlehem, there was no room for them in the inn—there was no place for them to stay. Eventually, they found a place with the animals, and Jesus was laid in a manger. An animal food bin was his first crib! The animals made room for Jesus to be born when all the other places in the world were full. They showed hospitality and welcome to the Holy Family.

In a similar way, the angels appeared to the shepherds with the good news of Jesus's birth. The shepherds lived out in the fields; there wasn't always room for them in town. But the angels told them that the good news of Jesus was for all people, not just for a few. The angels made room for the shepherds in their song, and reminded them that they were included in the story of God's love. What if we offered good news of welcome and joy to all people, like the angels did? And what if we created spaces where others felt welcome and safe, like the animals did?

There are times when it seems that there is no more room—when our tables are full, or all the seats are taken, or the positions on teams are filled, or the four-player game already has four players. But if we use our creative hearts and minds, we can always make a little more room for someone who might be feeling left out, or wants to join in. We can change the game a little to allow others to play, or take turns so that they have a chance to be a part of what's happening. Like the angels and the animals, we can create moments and spaces of welcome in the world.

BLESSiNG

God of Love,
Give me the creativity, compassion, and desire to create spaces of welcome,
and to include others even when it seems there is no room.
Allow me to be inclusive like the angels, and to be generous like the animals so that all feel welcomed and loved.
Amen.

KiDS TABLE TALK

● How can you make room for others?

- What does it feel like to feel welcome and included? How can you make others feel welcome and included?

- What is one of your favorite games? How can you creatively change the game to allow more people to play? Try to play your game with this new rule and see how much fun everyone has when more people are included!

DAY 7: CHRISTMAS DAY: LIGHT OF THE WORLD

SETTiNG THE TABLE

This is a time during your day when you can simply be—JUST AS YOU ARE! Take a moment to settle in. Place one hand on your heart and your other hand on your belly. Breathe in . . . breathe out. As you breathe in, remember that God is with you in this moment. As you breathe out, remember that God loves you so much!

Today is Christmas Day, and we are all celebrating that baby Jesus has finally arrived! This is a day for lots of celebration—as well as for sharing time with those we love. Jesus's life is a light in our world that helps us better understand God's deep love for everyone. Today, as we celebrate God's love born into the world, we also consider how each of us can shine God's love and light each day.

Shine your light, little star!
— DARYN STYLIANOPOULOS, "LITTLE STAR"

ISAIAH 9:2

The people who walked in darkness have seen a great light.

FOoD FoR THOUGHT

With all the candles now lit on our Advent wreath, the light is so warm and bright. That light can serve as a reminder of all the many sources of light around us, of their radiance and brilliance.

Stars are so bright that we can see them from billions of miles away. That's very far indeed! The sun is the closest star to our planet—the light of our world. It helps things grow and gives us warmth. It helps us know what time it is and where to go. The sun is necessary to all living things on our planet.

Some of the same materials and elements that make up stars are also a part of our bodies. And just like stars, we have light that we can share and shine in this world. Have you ever seen someone so full of joy that they seem to light up? Or noticed a warmth inside your heart when someone does something kind for you—or when you do something kind for someone else? And there are people you know who help you grow, and show you the way to go in life, and who make you feel loved. They are like stars in our world, shining their light.

Jesus was a light to many—he offered food to the hungry, and he showed kindness and love to people around him that felt left out and alone. Jesus's light shined brightly through the love he demonstrated in his living. We can do the same for one another: we can be bright lights, little stars, in the world.

You are radiant! Shine your light!

BLESSiNG

God of Love,
Help the light and love within me to shine brightly for the world.
Amen.

KiDS TABLE TALK

- What makes your heart light up?

- Where have you seen love lighting up the world around you this week? Was someone especially kind at school? Did you see a friend offer to help when someone got hurt?

- What are ways that you can shine kindness and love in your own school or community?

NEW YEAR'S TRADITIONS

SETTING THE TABLE

This is a time during your day when you can simply be—JUST AS YOU ARE! Take a moment to settle in. Place one hand on your heart and your other hand on your belly. Breathe in . . . breathe out. As you breathe in, remember that God is with you in this moment. As you breathe out, remember that God loves you so much!

Today is another exciting day in our Christmas season. It is New Year's Day! Today marks the beginning of a new year and new possibilities. As we reflect together today, we will consider new ways we can share God's love with others this year.

Better is possible. It does not take genius. It takes diligence. . . . And above all, it takes a willingness to try.

— ATUL GAWANDE[30]

PSALM 51:10
Create in me a clean heart, O God, and put a new and right spirit in me.

FOOD FOR THOUGHT

Often for the new year, people make New Year's Resolutions. A resolution is like a commitment to try a new thing. You hope for something new, and you have the opportunity to try to make it happen. The New Year is not the only time we can make a resolution. Every day is an opportunity to begin again, to hope again, to try again. Sometimes we make mistakes. Sometimes we fail. Sometimes we might not get it right the first time. But we can try again and again to get it right. We can hope for something better, and we can try to make it happen.

Sometimes we hope for something better within ourselves—we hope we can use kinder words, or hope we can be more caring to the people around us, our friends, and family. Maybe we hope to try a new activity, or get better at a skill we've been practicing. Whatever it is, offer your hope for the day and for this new year—name it for yourself and the world. As we strive toward better things, it makes our world a better place for everyone.

BLESSING

God of Love,
Give me the strength and courage each day to try to add more kindness, more compassion and caring to my life, so that little by little, the world can become a better place for everyone.
Amen.

KiDS TABLE TALK

- What is one thing you hope for in this new year? What are some steps you can take to make that happen—even if they are little steps—one small thing at a time?

- On a sheet of paper, write down: What is one thing you hope to learn this year? What is one thing you would like to share this year?

- Keep this paper so you can look back over it at the end of the year!

THANK YOU FOR JOINING US AROUND THE WELCOME TABLE!

We are so thankful that you could join us in our journey through Advent at The Kids Table. Our Advent series also includes another book of daily reflections, Advent at The Welcome Table, as well as our discussion and journaling guide, Advent Table Talk. When read together, this Advent series is designed to create opportunities for you to journey through each day of Advent in meaningful conversation with loved ones and friends.

You have listened to our stories and have hopefully shared some of your own with others. This is exactly what we had in mind when starting The Welcome Table project.

When dreaming up The Welcome Table, we wanted to create a space for growth and learning, for the expanding of hearts and minds, and for engagement across differences of perspective and belief. We wanted to bring people together to help create deep conversations and meaningful connections.

We are not alone in our desire for these things. We know it is a need in our world and in our communities. We are all asking similar questions: How do we bridge differences? How do we better understand one another? How do we bring people together authentically?

This kind of healing begins with personal relationships that change us and soften our hearts toward one another—that invite us to move closer to one another instead of farther away from each other.

We are honored that we have been able to be together with you in this Advent season and hope that you will continue to share your beautiful voices and to join us around The Welcome Table.

IF YOU WANT TO KNOW MORE ABOUT WHO WE ARE, VISIT US AT WWW.THEWELCOMETABLE.CO

NOTES

1   Roald Dahl, *The Minpins* (1991).

2   "Fr Ibrahim: Aleppo is 'powerless and fearful', prayers for peace during Advent," November 28, 2016, AsiaNews.it

3   Cristina Uguccioni, "Aleppo: Clashes Offset by Lights and a Plate of Sweet Grain," December 15, 2016, English.CLOnline.org

4   Dr. Seuss, *The Lorax* (1971).

5   "Wangari Maathai: Biography," GreenBeltMovement.org

6   Dr. Seuss, *Oh, the Places You'll Go!* (1990).

7   Nancy Tillman, *On the Night You Were Born* (2005).

8   "The Lion and the Mouse," *Aesop's Fables*.

9   Dr. Seuss, *How the Grinch Stole Christmas* (1957).

10   John Lennon and Yoko Ono, "Imagine" (song), lyrics at JohnLennon.com

11   Gary Allan, Hillary Lindsey, and Matt Warren, "Every Storm (Runs Out of Rain)" (song).

12   Oprah Winfrey, "What Oprah Knows for Sure About Hope and Finding Peace," May 2018, Oprah.com

13   "Oprah Talks to Maya Angelou," *O, The Oprah Magazine*, May 2013, transcript at Oprah.com

14   Patricia C. McKissack, *What is Given from the Heart* (2019).

15   Kristen Anderson-Lopez and Robert Lopez, "Into the Unknown" (song), lyrics at Disney.Fandom.com

16   Juan Felipe Herrera, *Imagine* (2018).

17 John Lennon and Yoko Ono, "Imagine" (song), lyrics at JohnLennon.com

18 Corinna Luyken, *My Heart* (2019).

19 Carol Connors and Ayn Robbins, "Someone's Waiting For You" (song), from Disney's *The Rescuers* (1977).

20 Victor Fleming, dir., *The Wizard of Oz* (1939).

21 @TheSingleWoman (Mandy Hale), tweet, August 23, 2014, https://twitter.com/thesinglewoman/status/503036469813186560

22 Erin Hanson, "Fly," in *Voyage: thepoeticunderground2* (2014).

23 George W. Cooke, "I've Got the Joy" (song), lyrics at hymnary.org

24 Grace Byers, *I Am Enough* (2018).

25 @DollyParton, tweet, July 15, 2019, https://twitter.com/DollyParton/status/1150810989031542784?s=20

26 Clement C. Moore, *A Visit from St. Nicholas* (1823); this poem is more commonly known as *The Night Before Christmas*.

27 Barbara Cooney, *Miss Rumphius* (1982).

28 Nancy Tillman, *On the Night You Were Born* (2005).

29 Jan Richardson, "And the Table Will Be Wide" (2012), ThePaintedPrayerbook.com and JanRichardson.com

30 Atul Gawande, *Better: A Surgeon's Notes on Performance* (2007).

ABOUT THE AUTHORS

We are "The Bunce Girls", or at least that is what we have been called most of our lives. Originally from Lexington, North Carolina, we were raised surrounded by music, justice, and faith. Our mother and both grandmothers were music ministers, our father was an attorney, one grandfather was a professor, and the other was the pastor of our church. Needless to say, we were constantly challenged to express ourselves in thoughtful and meaningful ways. Often that was through the use of our voices, whether through singing or just good, honest conversation - conversations that most often took place around the table. Most of our Sunday afternoons were spent gathered around an open table with family and friends where the food was plentiful, stories and laughter connected our hearts, and where the presence of each individual was held sacred. It's those moments that have inspired The Welcome Table.